S0-BQX-041

Fill-in-the-Blank
Plotting

Fill-in-the-Blank Plotting

A GUIDE TO OUTLINING A NOVEL

Using the Hero's Journey
&
Three-Act Structure

by

LINDA GEORGE

CRICKHOLLOW BOOKS

Crickhollow Books is an imprint of Great Lakes Literary, LLC, of Milwaukee, Wisconsin, an independent press working to create books of lasting quality and practical value.

Our titles are available from your favorite bookstore, online or around the corner, or from your favorite library jobber or wholesale vendor.

For a complete catalog or to order any title, visit our website: www.CrickhollowBooks.com

Fill-in-the-Blank Plotting
© 2009, Linda George

All rights reserved. No part of this book may be reproduced in any form or by any means without permission in writing from the publisher, except for brief quotation in an acknowledged review.

Cover Design by Philip Martin

ISBN-13: 978-1-933987-03-3

First Edition • Original Trade Paperback

Contents

To Outline or Not To Outline?

Some writers don't like to outline their novel in advance. They prefer to let a story unfold "naturally," then go back and revise as needed. They feel this lets them follow a story's most organic course; it frees characters and situations to explore their own directions. Outlines may seem static or too logical, overwhelming unexpected changes, reversals, and surprises that may not have occurred to an author in the outlining process.

However, a spontaneous approach has its drawbacks! Time is often wasted writing a story into a dead end, then having to spend much time backing up to rewrite large segments. An outline might have anticipated and worked out such glitches in advance.

Far worse is a chance of total failure. Without an outline, an author flirts with the danger that a work, despite much energy invested, never pans out and eventually must be abandoned.

A good outlining method, then, allows flexibility and creative "eureka" moments, while assisting the author by providing a structural underpinning, a reliable way to develop a sequence of scenes, characters, turning points, and dramatic surges that all add up and make sense.

This fill-in-the-blank method developed by author and writing teacher Linda George fits the bill. She combines two well-tested structures to create a blended approach. It is a platform for creativity: a practical trellis for the climbing vines of your creative story.

One striking benefit of using her method is the physicality of it. As you post or pin notes on your storyboards, you see shapes and connections. You can step back and look; you can step up and move ideas in an instant. You can scribble notes in odd moments and later paste them up with the others. You can color-code characters or sub-plots.

As you devise your plot, you experience the emerging organization of your novel as a real presence in your workroom. It stands there day and night, ready to receive a stray thought or glance.

All this is invaluable – and greatly lacking on a computer. Computers do many things very well – other things, not so well. The danger is that computers lead us to write in computer-channeled ways; instead of being a tool, they may form the walls of a new rat-maze for us to run about in, forgetting the creative energies that can be found in index cards, push pins, colored highlighter pens, and, yes, even scribbled handwriting. Free yourself from the machine and create a fluid, visual creature: your storyboard.

Speaking of posting notes (and rats), I recall reading how author Philip Pullman built a shed in his backyard garden as his writing workshop. The interior was furnished with a giant fake rodent, a Giant Rat of Sumatra (a prop inherited from some theatrical production). Pullman's favorite tool for plotting was an inside wall where he posted his scenes written on sticky notes. He would arrange and rearrange freely until the sequence worked well, creating a holistic understanding of the work, allowing him to carry complex threads throughout. His outstanding trilogy, *His Dark Materials,* won a good number of awards and solidified his place in the pantheon of great writers and storytellers.

His secret? Was it the Sumatran rat? Or was it the plotting story-board? You won't know until you try for yourself. This booklet recommends trying the storyboard first!

Philip Martin, series editor
Crickhollow Books for Writers

Introduction

A Simple & Flexible Method

Plotting has always been a dreaded task for most fiction writers, whether they're writing short stories, long stories, or novels. Facing a blank page with only a sliver of an idea intimidates, repels, and frustrates many excellent writers. Some are lucky; plots pop into their heads fully formed and ready to be committed to the page. But for those of us who have to work hard at turning an idea into a workable plot, that blank page can be as daunting as a form rejection letter.

After years of struggling with plotting, and years of teaching and giving my students fill-in-the-blank exercises and tests, I decided there had to be a way to plot a story by filling in the blanks. The method eluded me until I learned about two excellent plotting structures – the Hero's Journey and the Three-Act Structure – and learned how to combine them.

Because I was a predominantly right-brained writer, I didn't have a lot of success with either structure as long as I had to deal with them on paper. Anything visual was better than anything written. So, I decided to put the Journey and the Structure on the wall of my office so I could see it. I attached a big bulletin board to the wall, pulled out a package of 3" x 5" cards, and eventually came up with a method of plotting that has served me well for twenty years.

In this book, I'm going to show you my plotting boards, the twelve steps of the Hero's Journey, and how the Journey fits into the classic Three-Act Structure. I'll also show how color can help you track plot points, character development, subplots, and anything else crucial to the plot.

I know I'm not the only one to ever stick cards on the wall. And I'm not the only writer to ever use the Hero's Journey and Three-Act Structure to plot a story. My method is a combination of methods I've gleaned from other writers and books on writing that work for me.

The best part of this method is the flexibility. It's easy to insert or delete scenes, move them from one chapter to another, track how long it's been since a minor character appeared, spot instantly where the crucial tidbits are placed and whether they're all there.

As long as you stick to some basic rules, the plotting boards can be customized to whatever works best for you.

So, let's get started!

Chapter 1

The Two Plotting Boards:
A Quick Overview

To summarize my method, I use two bulletin boards in a two-step process to plan a plot. The first board is the Hero's Journey. For that board, I place my starting ideas on it, in the form of cards, physically pinning them onto the surface.

Then I step back and review the steps of the Journey to figure out what's needed. I keep at it, elaborating or changing cards, adding cards to fill in any missing gaps, and moving or replacing cards, until I complete the twelve steps of the Hero's Journey.

Then I move those cards onto a second board: the Three-Act Structure, which helps to organize that emerging outline into the structure of a novel.

Let's start with a quick overview of the two boards, then we'll look at each board in more detail in following chapters.

Board One: The Hero's Journey

Let's begin by looking at the Hero's Journey board, where you will start to arrange the elemental ideas for your story and brainstorm ideas to expand them into a full novel.

For the Journey board, start by making twelve labels, to be arranged in order along the left side of the board. These mark the steps of the classic quest of the hero found in mythological tales around the world and in many successful modern novels as well. (For several useful books on the Hero's Journey, see the brief Bibliography at the back of this booklet.)

To make these twelve labels, I like to use old business cards. You can use index cards cut to a similar size, or whatever you like.

Board One: Twelve Steps of the Hero's Journey

The Hero's Journey consists of twelve steps or significant events in a quest that forms a story that takes your hero out into the world, through a series of challenges, and back again.

1. Ordinary World
2. Call to Adventure
3. Refusal of the Call
4. Meeting the Mentor
5. Crossing the First Threshold
6. Tests, Allies, Enemies
7. Approach to the Inmost Cave
8. Ordeal
9. Reward
10. The Road Back
11. Resurrection
12. Return With the Elixir

The next page shows the structure of Board #1.

Ordinary World

Call to Adventure

Refusal of the Call

Meeting the Mentor

Crossing the First Threshold

Tests, Allies, Enemies

Approach to the Inmost Cave

Ordeal

Reward

The Road Back

Resurrection

Return with the Elixir

Board Two: The Three-Act Structure

The second board contains the Three-Act Structure, an ancient dramatic tradition presenting a story in three acts. This structure follows a simple and effective pattern. Act One introduces the characters and conflict. Act Two, the longest, develops the story in an escalating drama of twists and turns. Act Three brings the characters to their final confrontation, the climax, and on to the story's conclusion.

Although there are three "acts," I choose a total number of chapters for my book that is divisible by four to create this board. For instance, twenty chapters is a good number.

The reason: the first act constitutes 25% or one-fourth of the story. The second act constitutes 50% or one-half of the story. The third act constitutes 25% or one-fourth.

So it works to use any number of chapters, as long as the number divides evenly by four (8, 12, 16, 20, 24, etc.).

For illustration in this booklet, I'll use twenty chapters, the number of chapters I generally use in my novels. However, this is just for the initial planning. You may later wish to revise the final number of chapters as you get further into your story. Short chapters may be combined, or longer ones divided, depending on the nature of your plot and where events fall within that plot.

In a book with twenty chapters:

Act I begins with Chapter One.

Act II begins with Chapter Six.

Act III begins with Chapter Sixteen.

The next page shows the structure of Board #2.

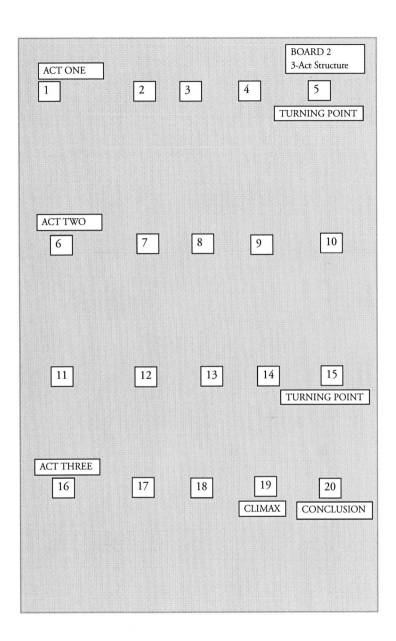

The Big Move:
Shifting Cards from Board 1 to Board 2

To combine the Hero's Journey with the Three-Act Structure, you will simply take the cards from Board 1 and move then to the appropriate slots on Board 2.

Here is your guide to roughly where the cards go.

Act I

Hero's Journey	Three-Act Structure
	(the step occurs in:)
Step 1	Chapter 1
Step 2	Chapter 2
Step 3	Chapter 3
Step 4	Chapter 4
Step 5	Chapter 5

Act II

Steps 6 and 7	Chapters 6–9
Step 8	Chapter 10
Step 9	Chapters 11–14
Step 10	Chapter 15

Act III

building suspense	Chapters 16–18
Step 11	Chapters 19
Step 12	Chapters 20

Clearly, there is some flexibility, but this is the basic structure to make sure your novel has the key steps and pacing.

Turning Points

The other points to mark on Board 2 are crucial dramatic points important to the Three-Act Structure.

Hero's Journey	Three-Act Structure
Step 5 ("Crossing the First Threshold")	First Turning Point
Step 10 ("The Road Back")	Second Turning Point
Step 11 ("Resurrection")	Climax
Step 12 ("Return with Elixir")	Conclusion

We'll discuss the role of these turning points, climax, and conclusion later. For now, simply label these important elements of the plot on Board 2.

When your boards are set up and marked with the designated "blanks," you're ready to start filling those blanks. First, though, let's look more closely at those key structures: the Hero's Journey and the Three-Act Structure.

Chapter 2

The Hero's Journey:
A Closer Look

J oseph Campbell's book *Hero of a Thousand Faces* details the element of myth in traditional storytelling. The twelve-step Hero's Journey evolved from this work. The story starts just before the hero/heroine (the main character) encounters the conflict or disaster or problem that requires attention. And it follows his or her story until that problem has been resolved in one way or another.

By identifying the twelve steps of the Hero's Journey for your main character, you ensure that all essential elements of the plot are present in your story. You also make sure that they proceed in a logical order: beginning, middle, and end.

Let's look at each step of the Journey and the essential part of the story each step contains.

As an example, we'll take a famous story – *Treasure Island*, by Robert Louis Stevenson – and use that to give a sense of the story element or scene if Stevenson were using a story board.

1. The Ordinary World
Your Main Character (MC) exists in an ordinary world. Whether or not he/she has a job, a vocation, a home, family, or only a desert island and a palm tree, that character is immersed in "life as usual." In writing fiction, that ordinary world, whether set in real-

ity or fantasy, exists as a backdrop to whatever crisis or problem will soon intrude on the MC's life and demand attention.

Establishing the ordinary world doesn't require a lot of words. The Main Character can be coming home from work when the conflict arises, or waking in the morning, or getting into a car or onto a plane, train, bus, or boat. Readers expect the ordinary world to be exactly that – ordinary.

This world for the Main Character is introduced in Chapter One, but the ordinary part of that world doesn't last long.

Treasure Island #1

> For Jim Hawkins, the Ordinary World is his life at the Admiral Benbow Inn where he lives with his mother.

2. Call to Adventure

Very soon, something happens to the Main Character that's anything but ordinary. Stories, after all, are about things that happen that are unusual and worth telling. They will cause the MC to move beyond the ordinary to be challenged to grow and become a true hero.

This precipitating incident is the event I like to call "the dead horse in the living room." Suddenly, there it is, a huge problem or situation. It is intruding, unavoidable, and perhaps in some way, intriguing or mysterious. We may not know how it got there, but it cannot be overlooked.

The Main Character might attempt to ignore the problem at first, but that horse is going to decay and cause all sorts of disease and filth for the MC – as well as a mighty stench. The horse must be dealt with before the MC can possibly return to "life as usual."

In the story you're writing, the conflict must be equally demanding and impossible to ignore. The MC cannot go back to the ordinary world without first tackling and resolving the conflict.

In most cases, this is not something the MC wants to do.

Wouldn't we all perhaps prefer life to be simple and not challenging? But without that call to adventure, where's the story?

Treasure Island #2

> The Call for Jim Hawkins comes when Billy Bones is given the black spot by Blind Pew, and knows he's going to die. He tells Jim about his chest – the reason he's being pursued. In essence, he gives the treasure map to Jim, with instructions.
> "... it's my old sea-chest they're after; you get on a horse . . . [and ride] to that eternal Doctor swab, and tell him to pipe all hands . . . . I'll share with you equals, upon my honour." (Chapter III)

3. Refusal of the Call

Still, the Main Character tries to figure out a way around this problem without actually getting in the middle of it. Maybe someone else will remove the dead horse from his living room. Maybe, the MC hopes, there are simple ways to solve the problem.

But no one else is willing – or able – to do it. Maybe the horse is only an illusion. Maybe. But the stench is real and getting worse by the minute. There seems to be no way to avoid dealing with this mess. But still, the MC tries – as most of us would – to find an easy way out. Maybe someone else will have an idea about how to get rid of the problem without the MC having to get his/her hands dirty.

Treasure Island #3

> Jim doesn't want the responsibility of Billy's chest. And leaving the inn is not what he wants to do. "The captain's order to mount at once and ride for Doctor Livesey would have left my mother alone and unprotected, which was not to be thought of." (Chapter IV)
> Jim's concern is defending the inn and his mother – not searching for buried treasure. What should he do?

4. Meeting With the Mentor

The Main Character confides in a friend or counselor or teacher or maybe a total stranger. The Mentor offers advice – or not. The Mentor agrees to help with the problem – or not.

Whatever happens, the Mentor's reaction to the problem leads the MC to realize that the issue must be faced. And to admit there's no way except to plunge straight into the problem and try to resolve it as quickly as possible.

Treasure Island #4

> Jim does as Billy requested and takes the oilskin packet containing the treasure map to Dr. Livesey and Squire Trelawney, thinking they'll take it off his hands and he can go home again. But they have other ideas after seeing what the packet contains.
>
> "'Livesey,' said the squire, 'you will give up this wretched practice at once. To-morrow I start for Bristol. In three weeks' time . . .we'll have the best ship, sir, and the choicest crew in England. Hawkins shall come as cabin-boy.'" (Chapter VI)
>
> There will be no going home for Jim Hawkins.

5. Crossing the First Threshold

At this point, the Main Character gathers whatever and whomever he needs to tackle the problem and sets out to get it resolved.

This is the point where the MC leaves the Ordinary World and enters the Special World, where he/she will remain until all has been taken care of and he/she is back home again.

This step of the Hero's Journey is a major turning point because the MC has left "life as usual." Without knowing it yet, he/she is about to embark on a series of grand adventures, in which anything and everything can – and will – happen before all is well again.

Treasure Island #5

Jim Hawkins meets Long John Silver and deems him a fine man, a good addition to the crew of the *Hispaniola*.

"I began to see that he was one of the best of possible shipmates." (Chapter VIII)

Captain Smollett, though, fears mutiny and is quite vocal about his disapproval of the crew Trelawney has hired. But ironically, Silver is trusted. Dr. Livesey tells Squire Trelawney:

"'. . . you have managed to get two honest men on board with you – that man [Captain Smollett] and John Silver.'" (Chapter IX)

6. Tests, Allies, and Enemies

Now the story enters the "dreaded middle" that all writers worry about. But the Hero's Journey doesn't allow for sagging middles. The Main Character has entered the Special World, where obstacles will be encountered on the way to the resolution of the problem.

The MC will hurdle some of these obstacles and go around or tunnel through others. Unfortunately, he/she will be defeated by some of them, suffering setbacks.

No matter. For every step backward, the MC makes some steps forward. This will lead him/her onward, believing the problem can be ultimately solved so he/she can go home again. It is not time to give up hope. There still are promising options – however difficult – that suggest a way toward a solution to the MC's problem.

Treasure Island #6

When Jim Hawkins takes a nap in an apple barrel, he overhears the pirates' plans to take over the ship – led by Silver. He knows in a flash their trust has been misplaced and they are all in grave danger. Jim tells Dr. Livesey, the squire, and Capt. Smollett. At least they'll know what's coming.

Jim gains new respect for the captain. "'We must

go on, because we can't turn back. If I gave the word to go about, they would rise at once. . . . what I propose is . . . to come to blows some fine day when they least expect it.'" (Chapter XII)

Jim is instructed to listen and report what he hears since Silver still considers him harmless. "I began to feel pretty desperate at this, for I felt altogether helpless . . . . there were only seven out of the twenty-six on whom we knew we could rely; and out of these seven one was a boy. . . ."

7. Approach to the Inmost Cave

We're almost to the middle of the story now, and the most challenging, ugliest test looms just ahead. This is a biggie. If the Main Character doesn't take care of this obstacle, there may be no hope for ridding him/herself of the conflict. The "cave" is not a literal cave in most stories, but is the image that describes the dark, fearful confines of the obstacle that threatens to surround and swallow the hero.

The MC has realized that the answer lies in going down an unavoidable path, even deeper into the Special World, to a location full of danger.

The MC gathers courage (and as many friends as possible) and enters the Inmost Cave – which proves to be the worst possible thing that could happen. The enemy is encountered, and a major battle ensues. This can be a battle of wits, fists, swords, bombs, or car chases, but it's a doozy.

This exciting struggle occurs in the middle of the story. No sagging middle for this book!

Treasure Island #7

Jim Hawkins goes ashore with the pirates, then sneaks away and meets an odd, half-crazed fellow, Ben Gunn, who was marooned on the island three years before. He tells about being on a pirate ship with a captain named Flint, who went ashore with six men to bury a chest of treasure, and came back alone. Long John Silver was on Flint's ship, and Ben fears him greatly.

Ben reveals an important tidbit: he has a boat, a crude homemade vessel!

The captain, doctor, squire, and loyal members of the crew take shelter in an old stockade, surrounded by the buccaneers. Silver arrives to offer them their lives in exchange for the map. The captain refuses the deal.

The next morning, the pirates attack. "Suddenly, with a loud huzza, a little cloud of pirates leaped from the woods on the north side and ran straight on the stockade. . . . the fire was once more opened from the woods, and a rifle ball sang through the doorway and knocked the doctor's musket into bits. The boarders swarmed over the fence. . . ."

Capt. Smollett is wounded and lives are lost, but they successfully defend the stockade. The pirates retreat to regroup for their next attack.

8. Ordeal

While the enemy may have been held off in an initial fight, the Main Character now has to face even more severe challenges. Often these are internal struggles as well as external, and the MC must face his/her own weaknesses or greatest fears. Through this, the reader will wonder, again and again, how the MC will ever avoid defeat to emerge victorious.

Often, after a dreadful struggle or ordeal, the MC will change in a significant way, in some ways being "reborn," transformed into a stronger character, more capable when facing the next set of challenges.

Surely, we hope, this will be the event that will open the door to home for the MC.

Treasure Island #8

Knowing they cannot withstand the pirates a second time, Jim decides to use Ben's boat, a flimsy skin coracle, to sabotage the *Hispaniola*. His plan is to cut the anchor and set the ship adrift, marooning the pirates on the island. But there are two men left on board.

In his tiny boat buffeted by the sea, Jim finally cuts the anchor rope, then struggles unsuccessfully to return to the island. Nearly swamped by waves, Jim cannot get back to shore, but re-encounters the drifting *Hispaniola*.

He scrambles on board to find one of the guards has killed the other in a drunken rage. Young Jim is chased up the rigging by the other savage pirate.

Cornered and injured by the pirate, Jim fires his pistols and kills the man attacking him.

Jim is victorious. The ship is his!

9. Reward

Miracle of miracles! The Main Character has won a great battle! It seems the foes have been defeated! The dead horse is surely gone from the living room now.

The MC celebrates. If you're writing a romance novel, this is the point where the first love scene should occur.

All appears well. It seems likely the MC will soon be free to go home again, once a few minor matters are wrapped up.

Treasure Island #9

The schooner drifts close to shore and comes to rest in an inlet. Jim makes his way back to the stockade, eager to tell the others about his great accomplishment.

"There lay the schooner, clear at last from buccaneers and ready for our own men to board and get to sea again. I had nothing nearer my fancy than to get home to the stockade and boast of my achievements."

10. The Road Back

The Main Character has traveled far and is deep in the Special World. It will take a long time and some effort to get back again to the Ordinary World – to the place where all is settled and calm.

But after all, the conflict has been resolved, right?

Wrong.

Setbacks occur. Ominous people, places, and events lead the MC to realize, to his/her chagrin, that the conflict may have been only temporarily quelled. Success is fleeting. The good that has been accomplished fades away. Perhaps a friend betrays the MC. Trouble is brewing again.

Suddenly, all the previous trouble comes back – and more!

Treasure Island #10

Jim returns to the stockade.

"All was dark within. . . . there was the steady drone of the snorers. . . . With my arms before me I walked steadily in. I should lie down in my own place (I thought with a silent chuckle) and enjoy their faces when they found me in the morning."

Jim discovers too late that the pirates have taken the stockade; he has fallen into their clutches.

11. Resurrection

Everyone or everything that has been fought in the past is back to fight again, but stronger or more intense this time, and with new weapons the Main Character may never have heard of or seen before.

The resurrection brings back every fear the MC ever had. From having to cope with a dead horse in the living room, now there is a whole herd more, crashing into the house and falling on the corpse of the first horse.

The MC is doomed. Emerging unscathed from this situation is nothing more than a frivolous hope at this point. There's no apparent way to win. The odds are now stacked mightily on the side of the enemy or the unsolvable problem.

It often happens that the MC will have to return to the place he/she least wants to venture again – back to the inmost cave – to once again face the enemy within.

The stakes are at their highest now, and chances of victory slimmest.

The MC might as well quit.

But this is the Main Character we're talking about!

It is impossible that he/she will ever give in and give up home, family, and happiness because of this conflict. This is why stories are told – to lift up heroes that find within themselves the strength to overcome even the greatest odds and the bleakest moments.

But the resolution, which *must* come from the MC, is likely not attained in the way he/she originally intended. Instead, a miraculous (but very human) effort occurs, orchestrated solely by the MC.

The MC must draw deep within to find a newfound strength and a way never imagined to defeat the enemy or problem. The crisis ends in a great climax. And the MC emerges victorious!

Treasure Island #11

They force Jim to go with them to find the treasure. As they follow the old treasure map, they encounter a grisly skeleton.

"[The skeleton] lay perfectly straight · his feet pointing in one direction, his hands, raised above his head like a diver's, pointing directly in the opposite."

When Long John, Jim, and the pirates find the place where the treasure was buried, it's gone! Ben Gunn dug up the treasure years ago and hid it in his cave.

The pirates squabble. The doctor and his men attack from the surrounding trees. Long John Silver once again changes sides and fires on his pirate comrades.

The doctor, Jim, and company escape to their rowboat. They journey around the island to Ben Gunn's large and luxurious cave, where the treasure lies.

12. Return With the Elixir

The Main Character, battered and bruised, but happy to have conquered the unconquerable, returns to the Ordinary World. This everyday life, though, will never be the same for the MC again.

Because of the trials, tribulations, and ultimate victory the MC has endured, growth has occurred in the MC. He/she is a better person for what's been experienced.

A happy and hopeful life is again possible – happier and more hopeful than ever would've been possible had the conflict never occurred. And the elixir – this prize above all expectation – allows the MC to lead a life much happier and more fulfilling than ever would've been possible had he/she never encountered the problem at all.

Treasure Island #12

Jim, Capt. Smollett, the squire, and the doctor haul the immense treasure to the ship.

Young Jim: "I was kept busy all day in the cave, packing the minted money into bread-bags.

". . . I think I never had more pleasure than in sorting them. English, French, Spanish, Portugese, Georges, and Louises, doubloons and double guineas . . . they were like autumn leaves, so that my back ached with stooping and my fingers with sorting them out."

On the *Hispaniola*, the victors sail and leave the pirates marooned – except for Long John Silver, whom they accept back into their midst. When they arrive at the nearest port, Long John steals a bag of coins, takes a small boat, and disappears.

Jim returns home to the Admiral Benbow and his mother, to dream of his adventures – hoping never to repeat them!

(On the next spread is the completed Hero's Journey storyboard for *Treasure Island*.)

Hero's Journey Storyboard
for Treasure Island

On the opposite page, then, is the completed Hero's Journey story-board for *Treasure Island*, filled out with the cards.

You can see that each step in the Journey is represented by one or more scenes.

Ordinary World	For Jim Hawkins, the Ordinary World is his life at the Admiral Benbow Inn where he lives with his mother.	
Call to Adventure	Billy Bones is given the black spot by blind Pew, it means he's going to die. He tells Jim about the chest – the reason he's being pursued.	He gives the treasure map to Jim, with instructions.
Refusal of the Call	Jim doesn't want the responsibility of Billy's chest. He is reluctant to leave the inn.	Jim's concern is defending the inn and his mother – not searching for buried treasure. What should he do?
Meeting the Mentor	Jim takes the oilskin packet with the treasure map to Dr. Livesley and Squire Trelawny, thinking they'll take it off his hands.	But they have other ideas after seeing what the packet contains. They want to get a ship and go in search of the treasure.
Crossing the First Threshold	Jim Hawkins meets Long John Silver and thinks he's trustworthy. But Capt. Smollett disapproves of the crew Trelawny has hired.	They set sail, with Jim along as cabin boy.
Tests, Allies, Enemies	Jim Hawkins overhears the pirates' plans to take over the ship – led by Silver. He realizes they are all in grave danger.	Jim tells Dr. Livesey, the squire, and Capt. Smollett. The captain says they must bide their time for the right moment to strike back.
Approach to the Inmost Cave	Jim goes ashore with the pirates, then sneaks away. He meets Ben Gunn, marooned on the island. Ben has a boat!	The officers and loyal crew take shelter in old stockade. The pirates attack. Captain is wounded but they defend the stockade.
Ordeal	Jim decides to sabotage the Hispaniola, using Ben's boat to cut the anchor and set the ship adrift.	The pirates will be marooned on the island!
Reward	Jim scrambles aboard the ship, but is wounded when he kills one of the pirates.	But he makes his way back to the stockade to tell the others about his victory.
The Road Back	Jim finds the pirates have taken the stockade. Jim is captured again. They force him to go with them to find the treasure.	Jim knows the minute they have it, all their lives will be forfeited.
Resurrection	When Long John, Jim, and the pirates find the place where the treasure was buried, it's gone! Jim's hopes of staying alive are renewed.	Ben Gunn dug up the treasure years ago and hid it in his cave.
Return with the Elixir	Jim, Capt. Smollett, squire, and doctor haul the treasure to the ship and leave the pirates marooned – except for Long John Silver.	At sea, Long John steals part of the treasure and a small boat, and disappears. Jim returns home to the Admiral Benbow and his mother.

Chapter 3

The Three-Act Structure:
A Closer Look

The three-act structure has been around a long time. Some writers prefer a five-act structure, but I've always found three acts to be all I can get my mind – and my plot – around. I'd read about the three-act structure but never understood it completely until I attended a two-day workshop with Linda Seger.

Seger's book, *Making a Good Script Great*, is one of the best resources I've ever found to deal with this classic structure. The book is geared toward screenplays, but that makes it no less valuable to the novelist or short-story writer because all good fiction follows the rules of the structure. Even a picture book follows the structure – with or without text!

The key to the three-act structure is placing crucial elements of the plot at crucial points in the whole of the story being told. Twenty chapters works well for me, so I'll be illustrating the various parts of the three-act structure within those twenty chapters.

Introduction

The introduction can take the form of anything that hooks the reader and pulls him/her into the story. It can occur in one sentence, one paragraph, or one scene, but shouldn't take up more than a few pages.

The introduction, ideally, should either introduce the crisis confronting the Main Character (MC) or hint at the crisis to come.

Act One

Act One begins when the Main Character encounters the dead horse in the living room – the problem or crisis that cannot be ignored. Action is demanded from the MC. In this act, which constitutes 25% of the story, the MC, at least one significant secondary character, and either the villain or the hint of a villain to come are introduced.

Try not to introduce too many characters in the beginning of this act, or the reader may become confused and stop reading. Agatha Christie got away with introducing twenty characters in the first chapter. I wouldn't recommend it for anyone else.

Treasure Island Act 1

Act One takes place in England, first at the Admiral Benbow inn, where the old sea-dog known as Billy Bones has taken refuge. He sings the song "Fifteen men on the dead man's chest," has young Jim keep an eye out for a "sea-faring man with one leg," and spins tales of pirates led by Captain Flint.

Billy is discovered by an old mate, Black Dog, and in fear for his life, Billy tells Jim to keep an eye on his sea chest. Billy is soon served a death threat, the black spot, and dies of a stroke.

Jim and his mother open the chest, find some doubloons and a bundle of papers, and flee. The inn is ransacked by a bunch of rough-looking men who trash the place looking for the missing contents of the chest.

Jim takes the papers to Dr. Livesey and the squire, Mr. Trelawney. The bundle contains two items: a log book and a treasure map of an island and its location. Livesey and Trelawney decide to buy a ship, gather a crew, and set off in search of treasure.

First Turning Point

The First Turning Point occurs at the end of the first act – in Chapter 5 of a twenty-chapter book. This key moment turns the action in a different direction. The first act indicated the story would run in a certain way. The first Turning Point, though, tells the reader, "Never mind what you thought the story was going to be about. It's become a new story. The story line has taken a sharp turn and cannot go straight ahead as before because of what just happened."

This event happens quickly and startles the reader. It is completely unexpected and typically adds an element of danger to the Main Character's life and handling of the crisis. It has now become a much more threatening crisis than before, and there's clearly no going back. The first Turning Point leads the reader into the next act.

Treasure Island, First Turning Point

The first turning point is the departure from England on the *Hispaniola*. In the almost 40 chapters of *Treasure Island*, this happens at the beginning of Chapter 10, with about 25% of the story told.

"I was dog-tired when a little before dawn, the boatswain sounded his pipe, and the crew began to man the capstan-bars. I might have been twice as weary, yet I would not have left the deck; all was so new and interesting to me – the brief commands, the shrill note of the whistle, the men bustling to their places in the glimmer of the ship's lanterns.

'Now, Barbecue, tip us a stave,' cried one voice.

'The old one,' cried another.

'Ay, ay, mates,' said Long John, who was standing by with his crutch under his arm, and at once broke out in the air and words I knew so well—

'Fifteen men on the dead man's chest—'

And then the whole crew bore chorus:—

'You—ho—ho, and a bottle of rum!'

And at the third 'ho!' drove the bars before them

with a will Even at that exciting moment it carried me back to the old 'Admiral Benbow' in a second; and I seemed to hear the voice of the captain piping in the chorus. But soon the anchor was short up; soon it was hanging dripping at the bows; soon the sails began to draw. . . ."

But the seeds of doubt are placed. Is Long John Silver and his motley acquaintances to be friends or foes?

The journey is underway. (In the Hero's Journey, this is "Crossing the First Threshold.")

Act Two

This act comprises 50% of the story. This is generally where the love interest subplot occurs, complicating the Main Character's life and quest even further. The pace may seem to slow a bit, even though the crisis continues to brew and grow all around the MC.

Halfway through this act, a momentous event occurs, requiring the Main Character to take action that hints at a resolution of the crisis. The MC is successful, and hope returns. A celebration ensues. This is generally where the first love scene also occurs, raising the stakes for the MC, who begins to wonder if all might be well in spite of remnants of the crisis remaining alive.

The MC longs for home, hoping the remainder of the problem will go away or take care of itself. But it isn't to be. By the end of the second act, the crisis has returned in force and is worse than ever.

Treasure Island Act 2

Act Two starts with the ship's voyage to the island. Jim, hiding in an apple barrel, overhears the seamen plotting with Long John Silver. On the ship's arrival at the island, some of the pirates are encouraged to go ashore.

Jim rashly slips in with them and then takes off to explore the island himself. He overhears Silver's evil plans, and then wanders about until he meet an odd castaway, Ben Gunn.

Meanwhile, Dr. Livesey goes ashore, finds an old stockade in good shape, and they decided to abandon the ship and take shelter there. They think the pirates will leave the island, with their plot foiled, and take the ship. But instead the pirates try to negotiate for the map. They won't leave without the treasure. Jim's friends refuse, and the battle is on.

At the midpoint of Act Two (the midpoint of the entire story), the author keeps the story hopping with a new adventure. Jim decides to take another independent outing, and slips away on his own again.

"This was my second folly, far worse than the first, as I left but two sound men to guard the house; but like the first, it was a help towards saving all of us."

His plan is to find Ben Gunn's crude boat, make for the *Hispaniola,* and somehow take over the ship. In a series of exciting adventures, he does manage to do just that, killing the last pirate on board.

Triumphant, he returns to the stockade in the middle of the night and slips into his bed, expecting to surprise his friends with the good news in the morning.

Second Turning Point

At the end of the second act comes the Second Turning Point. In a screenplay, this point is often referred to by the phrase, "Cut to the chase."

Whatever it is, the event that serves as the second Turning Point is a dark one. It proves without a doubt that whatever has been accomplished up to this point is for naught. The Main Character, the love interest, the secondary characters the MC cares about, are all in danger. No one but the MC can save them from imminent destruction.

Treasure Island, Second Turning Point

". . . it was like music to hear my friends snoring together so loud and peaceful. . . . All was dark within, so that I could distinguish nothing by the eye. As for sounds, there was the steady drone of the snorers, and a small occasional noise, a flickering or pecking that I could in no way account for.

"With my arms before me I walked steadily in. I should lie down in my own place (I thought, with a silent chuckle) and enjoy their faces when they found me in the morning.

"My foot struck something yielding—it was a sleeper's leg; and he turned and groaned, but without awaking.

"And then, all of a sudden, a shrill voice broke forth out of the darkness:

"'Pieces of eight! Pieces of eight! Pieces of eight! Pieces of eight! Pieces of eight!' and so forth, without pause or change like the clacking of a tiny mill.

"Silver's green parrot, Captain Flint!"

Jim is captured by Flint and his men. They took over the stockade when it was abandoned by Jim's friends.

Silver quells a rebellion; he has also gained the map. Act Two has taken some 20 chapters. The final act (the final 25%) will begin with Chapter 31: the pirates venture forth with the map to claim the treasure.

Act Three

This act contains the final 25% of the story. The pace is faster, thanks to the second Turning Point, with its impending disaster visited on the MC and everyone he/she cares about.

The action rockets ahead, leaving the MC and the reader breathless, turning pages faster and faster, desperate to know what's going to happen and how (or if) the MC is going to triumph when faced by overwhelming opponents and terrible odds.

Treasure Island, Act Three

The remaining six pirates set off across the island, heavily armed and carrying shovels. Soon they find an old skeleton, an omen, then hear a strange cry in the woods that terrifies the men till Silver realizes it is Ben Gunn. But when they reach the treasure site:

"A low cry arose. Silver doubled his pace, digging away with the foot of his crutch like one possessed; and next moment he and I had come also to a dead halt.

Before us was a great excavation, not very recent, for the sides had fallen in and grass had sprouted on the bottom. In this were the shaft of a pick broken in two and the boards of several packing-cases strewn around. On one of these boards I saw, branded with a hot iron, the name Walrus—the name of Flint's ship.

All was clear to probation. The cache had been found and rifled: the seven hundred thousand pounds were gone!"

Climax

The Climax of the story occurs in the final two or three chapters of the book. The MC has to make a life-changing decision in order to resolve the crisis and save him/herself and everyone else involved.

The resolution may or may not be what the MC and the reader have expected. Sometimes, having the expected happen is the worst possible thing for the MC. Sometimes, the MC cannot resolve the problem, but an alternative action presents itself and a solution is achieved that's best for everyone . . . if not what the MC and the reader wanted or expected to happen.

The crisis must be taken care of by the MC, without help from anyone unless solicited by the MC. It may involve an idea that startles him/herself and the reader, along with the villain and everyone else within earshot or sight.

Treasure Island, Climax

"There never was such an overturn in this world. Each of these six men was as though he had been struck. But with Silver the blow passed almost instantly. Every thought of his soul had been set full-stretch, like a racer, on that money; well, he was brought up in a single second, dead; and he kept his head, found his temper, and changed his plan before the others had had time to realise the disappointment."

Silver decides to turn tail and run. Jim's friends attack, firing on the pirates. In the attack, Silver and Jim run for it, "'Forward!' cried the doctor. 'Double quick, my lads." They dash for the boats. "And we set off at a great pace, sometimes plunging through the bushes to the chest. I tell you, but Silver was anxious to keep up with us."

Conclusion

After the Climax of the story comes the Conclusion, when the MC is allowed at long last to turn toward home, physically or metaphorically.

This time, the MC and the reader know that the MC will indeed reach home, unlike in earlier attempts to return that were foiled.

But the MC will return home a changed person, better for the experience in some ways, weary in others, but absolutely a different person with a new outlook toward life and the future.

Treasure Island, Conclusion

They escape to the boats, find the Hispaniola, adrift in a small harbor. They make their way to Ben Gunn's cave.

"And thereupon we all entered the cave. It was a large, airy place, with a little spring and a pool of clear water, overhung with ferns. The floor was sand. Before a big fire lay Captain Smollett; and in a far corner, only duskily flickered over by the blaze . . ."

. . . lies the treasure.

They load the boats, maroon the pirates on the island, but take Silver with them. When they reach the first port, Silver slips over the side and is gone.

"All of us had an ample share of the treasure, and used it wisely or foolishly, according to our natures. Captain Smollett is now retired from the sea. Gray not only saved his money . . . he is now mate and part owner of a fine full-rigged ship; married besides, and the father of a family. As for Ben Gunn, he got a thousand pound – which he spent or lost in three weeks, or, to be more exact, in nineteen days, for he was back begging on the twentieth. Then he was given a lodge to keep . . . and he still lives, a great favourite, though something of a butt, with the country boys, and a notable singer in church on Sundays and saints' days.

"Of Silver we have heard no more. . . .

". . . Oxen and wain-ropes would not bring me back again to that accursed island; and the worst dreams that ever I have are when I hear the surf booming about its coasts, or start upright in bed, with the sharp voice of Captain Flint still ringing in my ears: 'Pieces of eight! Pieces of eight!'"

(On the next spread is the completed Three-Act Structure storyboard for *Treasure Island*.)

Three-Act Structure Storyboard
for Treasure Island

On the opposite page, then, is the completed Three-Act Structure storyboard for *Treasure Island*, filled out with the cards, which have been moved here from the earlier Hero's Journey storyboard.

BOARD 2
3-Act Structure

ACT ONE

1
For Jim Hawkins, the Ordinary World is his life at the Admiral Benbow Inn where he lives with his mother.

2
Billy Bones is given the black spot by blind Pew; it means he's going to die. He tells Jim about the chest – the reason he's being pursued.

He gives the treasure map to Jim, with instructions.

3
Jim doesn't want the responsibility of Billy's chest. He is reluctant to leave the inn.

Jim's concern is defending the inn and his mother – not searching for buried treasure. What should he do?

4
Jim takes the oilskin packet with the treasure map to Dr. Livesey and Squire Trelawny, thinking they'll take it off his hands.

But they have other ideas after seeing what the packet contains. They want to get a ship and go in search of the treasure.

5
TURNING POINT
Jim Hawkins meets Long John Silver and thinks he's trustworthy. But Capt. Smollett disapproves of the crew Trelawny has hired.

They set sail, with Jim along as cabin boy.

ACT TWO

6
Jim Hawkins overhears the pirates' plans to take over the ship – led by Silver. He realizes they are all in grave danger.

7
Jim tells Dr. Livesey, the squire, and Capt. Smollett. The captain says they must bide their time for the right moment to strike back.

8
Jim goes ashore with the pirates, then escapes.
He meets Ben Gunn, marooned on the island. Ben has a boat.

9
The officers and loyal crew take shelter in old stockade. The pirates attack. Captain is wounded but they defend the stockade.

10
Jim decides to sabotage the Hispaniola, using Ben's boat to cut the anchor and set the ship adrift.

The pirates will be marooned on the island!

11
Jim scrambles aboard the ship, but is wounded when he kills one of the pirates.

12

13
But he makes his way back to the stockade to tell the others about his victory.

14

15
TURNING POINT
Jim finds the pirates have taken the stockade. Jim is captured again. They force him to go with them to find the treasure. Jim knows the minute they have it, all their lives will be forfeited.

ACT THREE

16

17

18
When Long John, Jim, and the pirates find the place where the treasure was buried, it's gone! Jim's hopes of staying alive are renewed.

Jim, Capt. Smollett, squire, and doctor haul the treasure to the ship and leave the pirates marooned – except for Long John Silver.

19
CLIMAX

20
Ben Gunn dug up the treasure years ago and hid it in his cave.

At sea, Long John steals part of the treasure and a small boat, and disappears. Jim returns home to the Admiral Benbow and his mother.

CONCLUSION

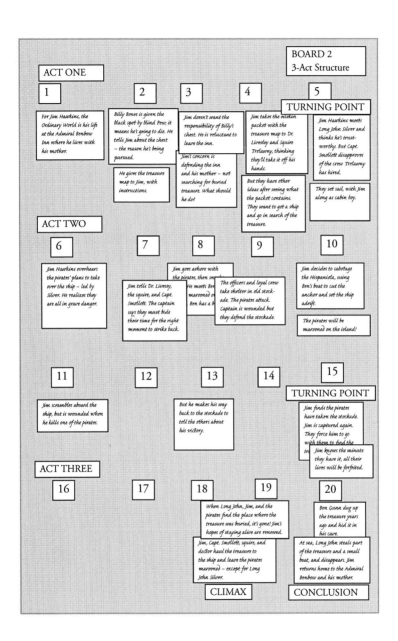

Chapter 4

Your Turn to Fill in the Blanks:
The Hero's Journey

Start with the Hero's Journey

Now it's your turn! You're ready to fill in the blanks for *your* novel (or story).

Begin with the Hero's Journey as structured on Board 1. Before moving ahead too far with the plot, make sure you have all twelve steps of the Hero's Journey for your Main Character well in place for the story you're going to tell.

I use 3" x 5" cards for filling in these blanks, with brief notations of each major event corresponding to each step of the Journey.

Usually, the first five steps require just one or two cards each. Then, as you move deeper into the Journey, you'll often find it will take more cards for each subsequent step.

The last steps may take up to ten cards each. Don't worry if this happens. It's natural for the plot to "thicken" as you move toward the climax scene, and for that climax scene to be the "thickest" of all the steps. However, the pace must move quickly.

The conclusion will happen briskly, needing only one or two cards.

Main Events Only

Remember that every walk the main character takes and every

conversation he or she may have does *not* have to be detailed in the Journey. *Only* those events that contribute directly to the resolution of the conflict – either moving positively toward that resolution, or being pushed back due to complications – are to be summarized on the cards for each step.

Once all twelve steps have been filled in, and the backbone of the story has been told, you're ready to move all the cards to the Three-Act Structure.

Chapter 5

Moving Cards to the Three-Act Structure

Act One

The first five steps of the Hero's Journey belong in the first act of the Structure, within the first 25% of the story. The first step (the beginning of the story in the "Ordinary World") typically will occur in the first chapter, if you choose to begin the story with "business as usual."

Or it may occur in the second chapter, if you choose to begin with action in a brief first chapter or a prologue, then step back to reveal the main character's ordinary world. Many suspense novels use this approach – first showing the killer commit a murder, and then switching to the main character, who will track down that killer in subsequent chapters.

The order of the first five steps of the Hero's Journey don't necessarily have to occur in 1-5 order, but most of the time they will.

Wherever they occur within the first quarter of the plot, be sure Step 5 ("Crossing the First Threshold") occurs at the end of the first act. This would be Chapter 5 in a twenty-chapter book.

This fifth step of the Hero's Journey is the entry point to the Special World, and serves as the transition to the second act of the Three-Act Structure. So it should happen as close to the second act as possible.

Act Two

The second act (Chapters 6–15) contains only a few steps from the Hero's Journey, but they are critical steps.

Step 8 ("Ordeal") should occur roughly in the center of the book, that is, in Chapter 10. This prevents sagging or slowing in the "dreaded middle." You want to keep the reader moving forward toward the third act and climax. The drama of the Ordeal should keep the reader fully engaged and fearing the worst.

Therefore, steps 6 ("Tests, Allies, Enemies") and 7 (Approach to the Inmost Cave") leading up to the Ordeal will occur somewhere within Chapters 6–9.

Steps 9 ("Reward") and 10 ("The Road Back") will occur somewhere within Chapters 11–15, with a strong transition to the third act occurring at the end of Chapter 15 (as the setbacks of Step 10 force the main character and friends back into the final showdown).

Act Three

The third act contains Steps 11 ("Resurrection") and 12 ("Return with Elixir"), with the Climax occurring within Chapters 18–20. The Conclusion comes at the end of Chapter 20.

The important thing to remember from this point on is that the steps of the Hero's Journey, now situated within the Three-Act Structure, are not set in cement.

Steps that must be in specific chapters are Step 5 at the end of Chapter 5 – the first turning point – and Step 8 at the mid-point of the book at the end of Chapter 10. In addition, Step 12 needs to happen as close to the end of the book as possible. You don't want to drag things on once the story is resolved. Finish quickly and on the relief following that high note.

The rest can be moved about and shifted somewhat – and probably will be, when you fill in the remainder of the plot.

Chapter 6

Preparing to Write Your Synopsis

Subplots & Secondary Characters

Once the "backbone" of the plot is in place, well distributed across the Three-Act Structure, it's time to add subplots, secondary characters, and the rest of the story to the board. Using more cards, put *only one scene per card*, then position them among the three acts.

This is where you'll have to move cards around, as you decide which scenes come before and after those backbone steps of the Journey.

You may at first end up with eight cards in one chapter and only two in the next. Feel free to step back, reconsider, and spread those cards out. Move them around, so each chapter is approximately the same number of scenes. But be sure to keep the key steps in their "must be there" positions.

Color Coding

To keep track of secondary characters or subplots, you may want to choose specific colors to flag the appearance of specific elements. I like to use colored index cards. That way, I can easily spot when the villain shows up, or whether or not I've mentioned a certain subplot in the past three chapters, or at which point a new character or subplot is introduced among the basic steps of the Journey.

Again, only those scenes that are crucial to the contribution or hindrance of the resolution of the conflict should be placed on the board. When writing the book, you'll be welcome to add incidental scenes wherever you like, but they don't all need to be on the board (or in the synopsis). When you've included *all* the *essential* scenes of the story on the board, you're ready to write the first draft of the synopsis.

Writing the Synopsis

To write your synopsis – a crucial run-through of the story's highlights in a form that often will be submitted with your manuscript for an editor to review – all you need to do is copy the cards into a single document, in narrative form, in the order you have them on the Three-Act Structure board.

Once the cards are all in the synopsis, go through and smooth the transitions between the scenes on the cards. Add transitions wherever needed and convert the individual steps, scenes, and acts into a flowing narrative, telling the story beginning to end.

If you come across scenes that don't flow naturally into the chronology of the story, you might consider deleting those scenes from both the board and the synopsis. Bumps in the smooth road of your story indicate more detail than needed for the synopsis. (Save those scenes, though, for possible use in the story or novel.)

When you've polished the narrative, you should have 5–10 pages, which is a standard-length synopsis. If your editor prefers something shorter, stick to the core twelve steps of the Journey for the synopsis. This will yield something closer to 3–5 pages. If your editor wants more detail, you can insert more scenes.

No matter the length, though, remember that a smooth-flowing narrative – delivered in *present* tense – is the goal for a good synopsis. If anything pulls the reader out of the story, it should be revised or deleted. The goal here is to tell the story to the editor as seamlessly and efficiently as possible.

Chapter 7

Writing the Book

The Path Is Clear

Now, you're ready to write the book. While it's not as easy as taking dictation, you have a lot of guidance to lead you from one scene to the next.

You know how many chapters you're going to have. You know what's going to be in each chapter and in what order. You know your subplots and secondary characters, where they'll appear and when they'll make a tidy exit.

You have a much better chance that all the loose ends will have been neatly tied by the time the climax is complete. Your first draft should be much stronger than if you simply started writing (and risked ending up down a side road with no room to turn around).

While writing, of course, you're free to move cards around if you find out the order you planned isn't working. It's not unusual. Often the need for this change is made clear by the cards and their order on the board. A scene needs to be shifted slightly among chapters in order for things to proceed smoothly.

How I Write

I use this fill-in-the-blank method when I start writing a new novel. My books generally begin with a snippet of an idea. My novel *Ask a Shadow To Dance* (Five-Star Books, 2005) began with an old newspaper clipping that I ran across while working on another project. In a few intriguing paragraphs, it told how a paddlewheel riverboat mysteriously disappeared from the Mississippi without a trace.

Since I love the imagination of stories based in the idea of time travel, I immediately imagined the panic of a character who found herself on that boat . . . knowing the vessel was going to disappear. What a great hook for a story! Sure enough, once I thought about it, ideas began to pop into my mind.

Instead of asking myself, "What if . . . ?" I usually expand that question to "Wouldn't it be *awful* if . . ." which works better for me.

Setting the book in Memphis, Tennessee, seemed logical to me, since the article noted that the boat that had disappeared had departed Memphis, headed for New Orleans.

Next, I began to imagine the details of a main character – a woman, since I'd be writing a time-travel romance.

My next task was to gather all the information I could find about Memphis in the 1880s. This is the decade I use for all my historical romances, a convenience since I can use my accumulated research and knowledge to avoid getting mixed up on clothing, customs, and other details.

I delved into books first, then when I was well prepared, I headed for Memphis for a site visit. I was able to learn things about Memphis from the people of that city that I never would have learned from a book or the Internet.

When I got home, brimming with information from wonderful people and with a stack of terrific books about the history of Memphis, I organized the research. As I read, bits and pieces fell into place in the story.

My heroine's primary conflict to find a way to stay off the riverboat headed for oblivion, without revealing what she knew to her family, and how she knew it was going to happen. The hero, from the modern era, was her source of information about the doomed boat.

Each time I figured out another piece of the puzzle, it went onto a handwritten card, then onto my Hero's Journey board. Eventually, the board filled with cards until I had a basic idea of the plot.

Once there was no more room on the Journey board, I knew it was time to move the cards to the Three-Act Structure Board – and then to write the synopsis, then the book itself.

As I worked through the rough draft, chapter to chapter, more cards were added to the board as ideas popped up. Some already there had to be discarded, while others were moved to find new places in the story. By the time I finished my first draft, the board was full of cards.

I knew that this first draft was far from being the final draft. So I started at the beginning again, studying the Three-Act Structure Board, looking at the ebb and flow of dramatic tension, sub-plots, elements of suspense planted to later be revealed. I edited. I revised. I added details from my research. A second trip to Memphis four months after the first filled in the gaps. The layers piled one on top of the other, adding texture, emotion, suspense, historical detail, and romantic tension.

Several months and several drafts later, I declared the manuscript to be finished and ready to submit.

Without filling in the blanks on my plotting boards, I have no doubt the process would've taken much longer, with a great deal more frustration. Of course, each writer must find the process/method/system that works best for him or her.

It is my hope that you will find something in my system that will work for you and help you along on your path to success as a novelist or a storyteller.

Chapter 8

Conclusion

Structured Flexibility

Plotting doesn't have to be a dreaded process for any writer. Structure is the key. This fill-in-the-blanks method will help you get a handle on the plot, filling in essential steps, turning points, and acts.

This structure should also help you summarize the plot succinctly and in a smooth narrative form. This makes it easy for an editor to see the meticulous work you have done to make sure your plot is complete in every detail.

The method is flexible enough to allow you to adapt to changing developments as you write, and allows your editor to make suggestions for revisions, which he/she will most certainly do. After all, that's the editor's job!

I no longer dread plotting. I hope my plotting boards will help you to feel better about the process, too, and more confident in transferring the story that's in your mind to the page – even if you change your mind every day!

TREASURE ISLAND
by Robert Louis Stevenson (1883)

The novel *Treasure Island,* originally titled *The Sea-Cook,* was published in book form in 1883, after an earlier serialization. It is a fast-moving adventure tale of pirates, buried treasure, maps, and tropical islands. The novel established the success of Scottish author Robert Louis Stevenson (1850–1894), who would later write popular works such as *Kidnapped, The Strange Case of Dr. Jekyll and Mr. Hyde,* and the poetry collection, *A Child's Garden of Verses.*

Treasure Island is mostly told from the point of view of young Jim Hawkins, balanced with the curiously unreliable character of pirate Long John Silver, with his distinctive peg leg and shoulder parrot, who plays the role of sometimes villain, sometimes ally. At age thirty, Stevenson began the novel on holiday with his family in a cottage in the Scottish Highlands; he wrote and read the first chapters aloud, soliciting suggestions from the family audience, young and old.

ACT I
1. Ordinary World
Jim Hawkins is a young boy who lives at his parents' inn, the Admiral Benbow, near Bristol, England, in the 18th century.

2. Call to Adventure

An old sea captain named Billy Bones dies in the inn after being presented with a black spot – an official pirate verdict of guilt or judgment.

Jim is stirred to action by the spot. He and his mother unlock Billy's sea chest, finding a logbook and map inside.

3. Refusal of the Call

Hearing steps, they leave with the documents before Billy's pursuers ransack the inn.

4. Meeting With the Mentor

Jim takes one of the documents to two friends, Dr. Livesey and Squire Trelawney. They recognize it as a map to a treasure buried by the pirate, Captain Flint, on a distant island.

Trelawny immediately plans an expedition.

5. Crossing the First Threshold

Trelawny is tricked into hiring one of Flint's former mates, Long John Silver, and many of Flint's crew. Only the captain, Smollett, is trustworthy.

The ship sets sail for Treasure Island.

ACT II

6. Tests, Allies, Enemies

Jim overhears Silver's plans for mutiny and tells the Captain.

Landing on the island, Captain Smollett gives the crew leisure time on shore, to trick the mutineers into leaving the ship.

Jim sneaks into the pirates' boat and goes ashore with them. From a hiding place, he witnesses Silver's murder of a sailor who refuses to join the mutiny. Jim flees deeper into the heart of the island, where he encounters a half-crazed man named Ben Gunn.

Formerly a member of Flint's crew, Gunn was marooned on the island with the treasure.

Smollett and his men go ashore and take shelter in a stockade built by pirates.

Jim returns to the stockade, bringing Ben with him. Silver visits and attempts a negotiation with the captain, but the captain is wary and refuses to speak to him. The pirates attack the stockade the next day. The captain is wounded.

7. Approach to the Inmost Cave

Jim sneaks off to hunt for Ben's handmade boat, hidden in the woods, and sails in it to the anchored ship. He intends to cut it adrift, marooning the pirates on the island.

He leaves the boat and cuts the ship's anchor rope, then realizes that Gunn's boat has drifted near the pirates' camp. The pirates do not spot him.

He floats around the island until he catches sight of the ship drifting wildly, and struggles aboard.

8. Ordeal

One of the watchmen, Israel Hands, has killed the other watchman in a drunken fit.

Jim takes control of the ship, but Israel turns against him. Jim is wounded but kills Israel.

9. Reward (Seizing the Sword)

Jim returns to the stockade. It's occupied by the pirates! Silver takes Jim hostage and tells him the captain has given over the pirates' map, provisions, and the stockade in exchange for their lives.

Jim realizes Silver is having trouble controlling his men, who openly accuse him of treachery.

Silver proposes to Jim that they help each other by pretending Jim is a hostage. But the other pirates present Silver with the black spot. He's no longer their commander.

Silver pulls out the treasure map and leads his men and Jim to the site of the treasure.

10. The Road Back

The treasure's gone!

Dr. Livesey, Bun Gunn, and the others fire on the pirates, who scatter throughout the island.

ACT III

11. Resurrection

Jim and Silver flee and are guided to Ben's cave, where Ben hid the treasure, months before.

12. Return With Elixir

After spending three days transporting the loot to the ship, they prepare to sail for home. The Captain leaves the mutinous pirates marooned on the island, but Silver is allowed to board the ship. He sneaks off the ship one night with a portion of the treasure and is never heard from again.

They return home with the remaining treasure. Captain Smollett retires from the sea and Ben becomes a lodge-keeper.

Jim swears off treasure-hunting forever, dreaming about his adventures on Treasure Island, the sea, and gold coins.

CHARLOTTE'S WEB
by E. B. White (1952)

Charlotte's Web, the beloved children's book by E.B. White, was published in 1952, and became one of the best-selling children's book of all time. E.B. White (1899–1985, born Elwyn Brooks White) is also renown as the co-author of the writing handbook *Elements of Style* with William Strunk, Jr. For that guide, White took an earlier work by his professor at Cornell and revised it. The slim guide advocates clear and elegant prose.

White's other famous children's books include *Stuart Little* and the *Trumpet of the Swan.*

Charlotte's Web tells the charming story of Charlotte, a spider, and her friendship with Wilbur, a pig.

ACT I
1. Ordinary World
Fern Arable lives on a farm with her parents, who raise pigs.

When a runt is born, Fern pleads with her father not to kill it. He concedes. She names the pig Wilbur and cares for him like a pet. When he's five weeks old, and too big for Fern to care for, they take Wilbur to a farm owned by Fern's uncle and aunt, Homer and Edith Zuckerman. Fern visits him almost every day.

2. Call to Adventure

Wilbur is unable to see Fern every day, and is rejected by the other farm animals.

3. Refusal of the Call

Wilbur is lonely and longs for a friend.

4. Meeting With the Mentor

One night, Wilbur hears a tiny voice, saying, "I'll be a friend to you. I like you."

5. Crossing the First Threshold

At daybreak, Wilbur identifies the voice as that of a gray spider named Charlotte, who spins her web in the doorway of the pen. They become friends, and Wilbur isn't lonely anymore.

Wilbur grows bigger and bigger. Life is good until a sheep tells him that Farmer Zuckerman is planning to fatten him up and kill him at Christmastime.

Wilbur is terrified! He pleads for help.

ACT II

6. Tests, Allies, Enemies

Charlotte tells Wilbur she'll find a way to spare him from being killed for Christmas Dinner. She works throughout the night.

The next morning, Lurvy, the hired hand, comes to feed Wilbur and notices Charlotte's web, sparkling with dew. Clearly woven in the center of the web are the words SOME PIG.

It's declared a miracle. This surely is SOME PIG. A special pig. Only Mrs. Zuckerman seems to think the only thing special is the spider.

It would seem Wilbur has been saved – for the moment.

A few days later, Charlotte calls a meeting of all the animals to make suggestions for another message to be woven into the web. The goose suggests TERRIFIC. Everyone agrees it's perfect – except Wilbur, who doesn't feel terrific. Charlotte assures him that's okay because humans believe everything they read, whether it's the truth or not.

Charlotte weaves TERRIFIC in the web.

Another miracle on the Zuckerman farm! He has a large crate built with gold letters on the side saying, "Zuckerman's Famous Pig." In September, Wilbur will ride in the crate to the County Fair.

Charlotte knows she can't quit yet. She convinces the rat, Templeton, to bring her some paper back from the dump with some writing on it. After all, Wilbur's slops are a large part of Templeton's food, too. He agrees and returns with a piece of paper from a box of soap flakes. The words say, "With New Radiant Action."

Charlotte decides Wilbur is, indeed, RADIANT, and weaves the word into her web.

7. Approach to the Inmost Cave
On the first day of the fair, Wilbur is bathed in buttermilk and readied for the fair. Charlotte and Templeton get into the crate, too, to go with Wilbur to the fair.

Charlotte needs to stay home and weave her egg sac, but she doesn't feel Wilbur will be able to deal with the fair on his own.

8. Ordeal
When Wilbur is unloaded, Mr. Arable tells Mr. Zuckerman, "You'll get some extra good ham and bacon, Homer, when it comes time to kill that pig."

Winning a prize at the fair seems to be Wilbur's only hope to stay alive.

Charlotte tells Templeton, bloated from eating scraps at the fair, to bring her one last word – the last word she'll ever weave.

Templeton brings back a newspaper clipping with the word HUMBLE.

Charlotte weaves HUMBLE into her web.

Charlotte is weak and shrunken, near death. She has woven an egg sac and wishes she could've lived to see her children.

Everyone arrives at the pen and sees HUMBLE written in the web. Another miracle!

Then, Avery points to a blue ribbon – on the pig's pen next to Wilbur's. Wilbur didn't win anything. So what will happen to him now?

9. Reward (Seizing the Sword)

The loudspeaker rings with an announcement for Mr. Zuckerman to come to the judges' booth to accept a special award of $25 and a medal for his exceptional pig.

Alone at last, Wilbur asks Charlotte, "Why did you do all this for me? I don't deserve it. I've never done anything for you."

Charlotte replies lovingly, "You have been my friend."

10. The Road Back

Charlotte tells Wilbur she's too weak to go back to the farm with him. In two days, she'll be dead. Wilbur is heartbroken. He gets Templeton to cut down the egg sac and takes it gently into his mouth to ride on his tongue back to the farm.

Wilbur is put back in the crate. He winks at Charlotte. She knows her children are safe.

"Charlotte was alone when she died."

ACT III

11. Resurrection

Back at the farm, Wilbur watches over the egg sac through the winter. In the spring, hundreds of tiny spiders crawl out of the sac, run all over the place, then, on a warm, windy day, form little balloons with their spinnerets and float away. Wilbur, frantic, yells, "Come back, children!" But this is their chance to enter the world and spin webs for themselves.

12. Return With Elixir

Wilbur, thinking all are gone, is thrilled when he hears three voices, from three of Charlotte's daughters, on three webs in the doorway where Charlotte used to live. Now, Wilbur will never be slaughtered, and he'll never be lonely again.

Mr. Zuckerman takes good care of Wilbur for the rest of his days. No one ever forgets the miracle of the web. And Wilbur never forgets Charlotte.

GONE WITH THE WIND
by Margaret Mitchell (1938)

G*one with the Wind,* a Civil War romance, by Margaret Mitchell (1900–1949), was published in 1936. It won a Pulitzer Prize the following year.

A columnist for the *Atlanta Journal,* Mitchell wrote a number of character sketches, including profiles of Southern Civil War generals. A gifted writer, she is reported to have begun *Gone with the Wind* when nursing a broken ankle, as a diversion. She worked on it over many years, until the stacked manuscript was taller than she was.

The character of blockade runner Rhett Butler is said to be based in part on her first husband. The fiery romance between Scarlett O'Hara and Butler, along with her love for her home in Georgia, called Tara, set against the backdrop of life on a Southern plantation spanning the years from before to after the tumultuous war, has struck a chord in readers for decades.

ACT I

1. Ordinary World

Scarlett O'Hara, heir to the plantation home, Tara, is constantly surrounded by admirers, but her heart belongs only to Ashley Wilkes.

2. Call to Adventure

Her heart breaks when she learns that Ashley is engaged to his cousin, Melanie Hamilton.

3. Refusal of the Call

She declares her love to Ashley, but to no avail.

4. Meeting With the Mentor

Rhett Butler eavesdrops on her declaration, angering Scarlett. He tells her she should forget about Ashley Wilkes, since he's around and interested in her.

She ignores Rhett's interest and decides to punish Ashley by marrying Charles Hamilton the day after Ashley and Melanie are wed. But Charles is killed in the war, leaving Scarlett a widow.

5. Crossing the First Threshold

Scarlett moves to Atlanta to stay with Melanie.

ACT II

6. Tests, Allies, Enemies

Scarlett sees Rhett Butler again at a charity ball. Rhett pays $150 to dance with Scarlett, who is still dressed in black to mourn Charles. This act – dancing while in mourning – creates a scandal. Afterward, Rhett visits her regularly.

The South begins to crumble. Deaths mount. Scarlett works as a volunteer nurse and lives only to read the casualty lists every day, praying not to find Ashley's name. Ashley comes home for a brief leave, battered by war, and makes Scarlett promise to watch over Melanie when he has to return to the fighting. Melanie is pregnant.

When Melanie's baby is born, Scarlett has to deliver the baby without help, in the midst of chaos when their home is attacked by Yankees.

Scarlett meets Big Sam, formerly slave foreman at Tara, and learns that her mother is ill.

7. Approach to the Inmost Cave

The Yankees burn Atlanta while the Confederates retreat. Rhett helps Scarlett, Melanie, and the baby flee the city and leaves them on the road to Tara.

He gives Scarlett his gun, kisses her goodbye, and returns to Atlanta.

8. Ordeal

The women return to Tara. Scarlett's mother is dead. Her father is helpless. Tara lies in ruins. Scarlett, starving, digs up a turnip and hungrily eats it. Rising, she shakes her fist at the war, at all of her misfortune and vows, with God as her witness, she'll never be hungry again.

9. Reward (Seizing the Sword)

Scarlett restores Tara to productivity and joins the slaves picking cotton in the fields. When she discovers a Yankee deserter trying to loot Tara, she kills him with Rhett's gun and takes the money he's stolen from others.

Frank Kennedy asks Scarlett for her permission to marry Scarlett's younger sister, Suellen. Scarlett gives her consent.

10. The Road Back

Then, Scarlett learns that taxes on Tara have been raised to $300 – an impossible amount.

Again, Scarlett meets Ashley in secret, declaring her love for him, begging him to run away with her. But Ashley declines, telling her she could never leave Tara and the land she loves.

Tara's former overseer offers to buy Tara, but Scarlett refuses. Her father, on his horse, tries to chase the overseer away. Mr.

O'Hara falls and dies.

Scarlett has no choice. She goes to Atlanta to seek help from Rhett, but he's a prisoner, jailed for blockade running and war profiteering. His money is tied up in Europe.

On the way home, Scarlett runs into Frank. She tells him Suellen cannot marry him because she's engaged to another man – but Scarlett can marry him. And, she does, to get the tax money. She uses Frank's money to build a mill and shames Ashley into working there.

When Scarlett is attacked by hobos on her way to the mill, Frank, Rhett, who has been released from prison, and Ashley go looking for the attackers. Frank is killed. Ashley is injured.

ACT III
11. Resurrection

Rhett asks Scarlett to marry him and she finally says yes. They move to Atlanta and have a daughter, Bonnie Blue. Scarlett tells Rhett there will be no more children because she's still in love with Ashley. Rhett leaves, but returns soon, unable to stay away from Bonnie. After getting drunk one night, Rhett carries Scarlett to bed, determined to drive Ashley from Scarlett's mind forever.

The next morning, Rhett leaves with Bonnie, for London. When he takes Bonnie home to visit her mother, Scarlett admits she's pregnant, but doesn't want the baby. Scarlett accidentally falls down the stairs and loses the baby.

Later, sitting on the porch, Bonnie rides her pony and suddenly declares she's going to jump. She does and falls. She dies. Rhett goes mad with grief, shoots the pony, and temporarily refuses to allow them to bury Bonnie.

Melanie, pregnant again, collapses. She asks Scarlett to look after Beau, their son, and to be kind to Ashley. Melanie dies. When

Scarlett sees how stricken Ashley is over Melanie's death, she realizes he really loved Melanie all along. Not Scarlett.

12. Return With Elixir

She knows, finally, that she and Ashley will never be together. She also realizes that she really loves Rhett and rushes home to tell him.

She finds Rhett packing to leave her – for good this time. She begs him not to go and asks what she'll do without him. Rhett tells her, "Frankly, my dear, I don't give a damn," and leaves.

Scarlett realizes she must go home to Tara. There, she'll figure out a way to get Rhett back.

After all, "Tomorrow is another day!"

Bibliography

Linda Seger, *Making a Good Script Great* (Samuel French, 2nd edition, 1994). One of the great books on screenwriting and how to structure a story.

Christopher Vogler, *The Writer's Journey: Mythic Structure for Writers* (Michael Wiese, 3rd edition, 2007 paperback). Looks at archetypal heroes and the struture of their journey, and shows how the structure is used in many popular movies.

Joseph Campbell, *The Hero with a Thousand Faces* (Princeton University Press, reprint edition, 1972). The ground-breaking work that drew attention to the universal power and appeal of the mythic hero's journey that appears in traditional tales around the world.

About the Author

Linda George is an experienced professional writer, well known throughout the Southwest for her coaching of beginning writers via her website and in workshop settings.

She has written and published numerous books and articles. Her novels include *Gabriel's Heart* (under the penname Madeline George), *Ask a Shadow to Dance,* and *Silver Lady.* She and her husband Charles have more than sixty nonfiction books for children and teens to their credit. They live in West Texas.

For more information, or to schedule a writers' workshop based on *Fill-in-the-Blank Plotting,* visit the website:

www.charlesandlindageorge.com